Where the River Flows

McDougal & Associates
Servants of Christ and Stewards of the Mysteries of God

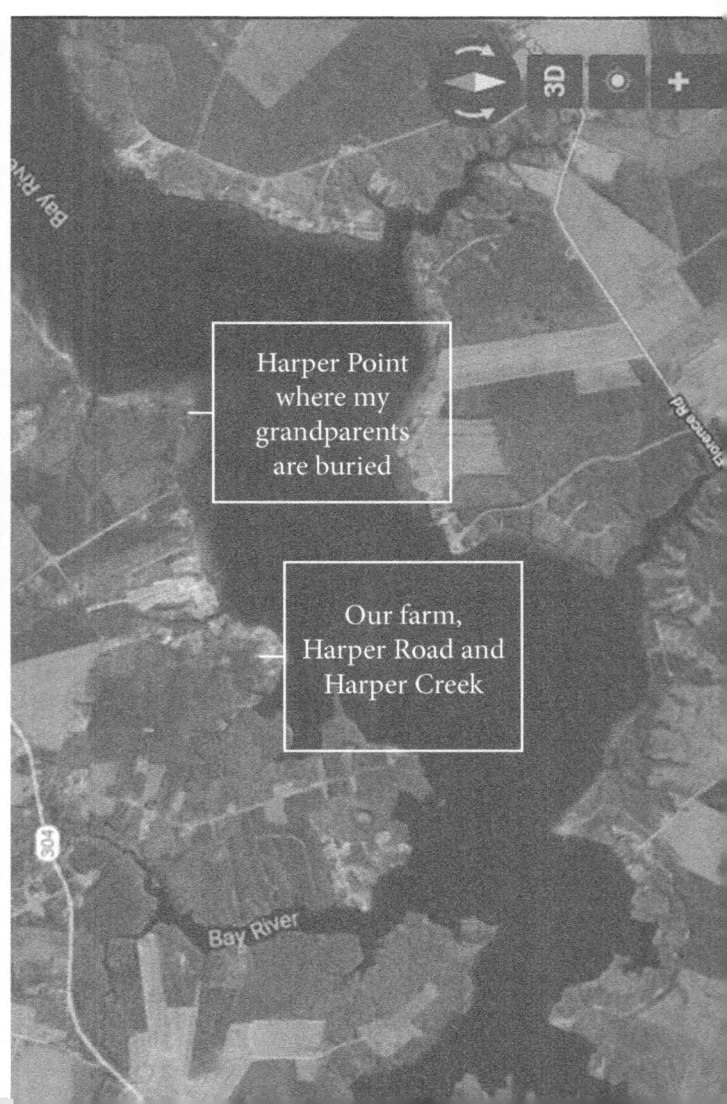

Harper Point
where my
grandparents
are buried

Our farm,
Harper Road and
Harper Creek

Bay River

304

Bay River

Where
the River
Flows

by

Phyllis Harper Isenhart

WHERE THE RIVER FLOWS

Published by:
McDougal & Associates
18896 Greenwell Springs Road
Greenwell Springs, LA 70739
www.thepublishedword.com

McDougal & Associates is dedicated to the spreading of the Gospel of Jesus Christ to as many people as possible in the shortest time possible.

ISBN 978-1-950398-01-0
Printed on demand in the US, the UK and Australia
For Worldwide Distribution

Dedication

I dedicate the book to my Redeemer and the one true Lover of my soul, Jesus Christ. He is the one who left the ninety and nine to go fetch me out of the mess I had made of my life. He is the one who planted me in His river of love and has sustained me all these years. He is the only one who loves me unconditionally. He is the one who brings peace to the storms of life and healing to a body wracked with disease and pain.

He is the one who inspired me to write my story, revealing His Spirit in ways I could never have imagined. I thank Him for His river of love that sustains and feeds my soul and so dedicate the work to Him – Jesus Christ the one true Source of Life.

Acknowledgments

There have been many down through the years who have inspired me. I would like to acknowledge a few of them.

My father, Rev. Elmo Harper: He was the person I always looked up to and admired the most. The many days and hours we spent together, especially on the river, provided a backdrop for this book.

Rev. Gaylon Benton and his wife, Barbara: You were mentors to me and taught me so very much of what it means to live in the Spirit. Thank you for answering God's call.

Francis Nethercutt: My long-time friend, you spent many hours editing and proofing this work. As a former English teacher, your expertise was deeply appreciated. Thank you so very much.

Contents

There Is a River

There is a river, and it flows from deep
within.
There is a fountain, that frees the soul
from sin.
Come to this water; there is a vast supply.
There is a river, that never shall run dry. [1]

The River Is Here

Down the mountain the river flows.
And it brings refreshing wherever it goes.
Through the valleys and over the fields,
The river is rushing and the river is here.

Chorus:
The river of God sets our feet a dancing.
The river of God fills our hearts with cheer.
The river of God fills our mouth with laughter.
And we rejoice, for the river is here.

The river of God is teeming with life,
And all who touch it can be revived.

And those who linger on this river's shore
Will come back thirsting for more of the Lord.

Up to the mountain we love to go
To find the presence of the Lord.
Along the bank of the river we run.
We dance with laughter, giving praise to the Son.[2]

2. Written by Andy Park. Copyright © 1994 by Mercy/
Vineyard Publishing (ASCAP). Used By Permission.

Introduction

As a child I would sit on the banks of the river, many times with my dad, and watch as it flowed past. We were blessed to live on a fifty-acre farm, located on a peninsula and surrounded on three sides by water. Our house sat in the middle of the property and we could see the river from there.

In the summer, Dad and I would often rise early and go

to the river to fish and crab. I was fascinated with the water.

Saturday afternoon, especially in the summertime, was family time, and we would all go to the river to swim.

As I grew older, I began to realize why I loved the river so much. There was a solitude and quietness about it. I found peace and contentment on the banks of that river. There was also joy and laughter. What is there about water, be it a river or an ocean, that can quiet the spirit and bring refreshing?

The Bible talks a lot about rivers and likens the Holy Spirit to

Introduction

a flowing river. So, where does a river have its beginnings? Most rivers start from high up in the mountains.

As the spring sun brings warmer temperatures, the ice and snow of winter begin to melt. The fresh water that results then begins its journey by winding and twisting its way down the mountainside. It will always take the path of least resistance.

As the stream trickles down, gaining momentum and volume, it also picks up speed and becomes stronger and more

15

powerful. It can even etch out crevices in the face of the mountain. As it travels downward, the water will get ever deeper and wider, until it reaches its destination. It will even join with other streams, although sometimes creeks or other little tributaries will branch off and go their own way.

Well, life is a lot like a river, and God has a wonderful river of life that He offers to each of us. This is my story.

Phyllis Isenhart
Jacksonville, North Carolina

The River of God

He that believeth on me, as the scripture hath said, out of his belly shall flow rivers of living water.   John 7:38

A river, in the natural sense, is a body of water that is flowing. In other words, it is constantly moving. In a natural river, there are all kinds of life. These can vary in size from microscopic plankton to huge fish. But what about in the spiritual sense? What is a spiritual river?

God is a Spirit and He is om-nipresent, meaning ever-present or always present. "Okay," you might say, "what, then, is the River of God?" If a natural river water is flowing in the earth, for God, we, His people, become the earth that His water flows through.

What is God's water? It is His Spirit. We, then, must allow His Spirit to flow through us. Just as the natural earth forms the banks of a natural river, you and I form the banks for the River of God to flow through.

The River of God

What other ways do the natural and spiritual rivers compare? There are many things found in and around a natural river, things like fish, crabs, shrimp, oysters, and all of these are beneficial to us. There are plants on the banks of a river, especially trees and grass.

Often what we call marshlands can be found along rivers. In these marshy areas many types of birds live. Certain birds, in fact, are only found near bodies of water. These would include seagulls and pelicans near salty water and others near fresh water: bitterns, coots, cranes, ducks, geese and flamingos, just to name a few.

Just as a natural river attracts much life, so it is with the River of God. His River is rich with things that are beneficial to our spiritual lives. What, for instance? Well, look at what John recorded Jesus as saying: *"He that believeth on me, as the scripture hath said, out of his belly shall flow rivers of living water."* Exactly what did Jesus mean by this?

As I said, when I sat on that river bank as a child, I experienced peace and contentment. And the same is true of God's River. In the midst of the hustle and bustle of everyday life, we can get away and find peace and contentment sitting on the banks of His River, sitting in the presence of His Spirit.

In God's River, there is solace, there is rest and there is refreshing. As we jump into His River, we can begin to swim in His goodness, be cleansed by His forgiveness and be renewed and refreshed in our spirit.

Just as there is a necessity in life for the water of a natural river, so there is a necessity in our lives for the spiritual River of God to be allowed to flow. But it is up to us where and how we let that fiver flow in and through us. God is the perfect gentleman, and He will not force Himself on or us. He leaves to us how much of Him we want.

Someone might ask, "What exactly is this River of God you are talking about?" Isaiah spoke of it:

> For I will pour water on the
> thirsty land,
>   and streams on the dry
>   ground;
> I will pour out my Spirit on
> your offspring,
>   and my blessing on your de-
>   scendants.

22

The River of God

*They will spring up like grass
in a meadow,
like poplar trees by flowing
streams.*

Isaiah 44:3-4, NIV

Ezekiel also spoke of the River of God. God showed him the River issuing out from under the door of the Temple in Jerusalem. Ezekiel saw a man with a measuring line in his hand, and the man measured off a thousand cubits (about three tenths of a mile) out from the Temple gate facing east. At that point, the water was just a trickle.

Then the man led Ezekiel out further, and the water rose to his ankles. He then led Ezekiel out another thousand cubits, and the water was now up to the prophet's knees. They went still another thousand cubits, and the water was now waist deep. Finally, they went another thousand cubits, and the water was now deep enough to swim in but too deep to cross over.

The man then took Ezekiel back to the bank of the River and showed him all the goodness that grows in the River and along its banks. Ezekiel ended the telling of his vision with these words:

The River of God

He said to me, "This water flows toward the eastern region and goes down into the Arabah [the Jordan Valley], where it enters the Dead Sea. When it empties into the sea, the salty water there becomes fresh. Swarms of living creatures will live wherever the river flows. There will be large numbers of fish, because this water flows there and makes the salt water fresh; so where the river flows everything will live.

"Fishermen will stand along the shore; from En Gedi to En Eglaim there will be places for spreading nets. The fish will be *of many kinds — like the fish of the Mediterranean Sea. But the swamps and marshes will not become fresh; they will be left for salt. Fruit trees of all kinds will grow on both banks of the river. "Their leaves will not wither, nor will their fruit fail. Every month they will bear fruit, because the water from the sanctuary flows to them. Their fruit will serve for food and their leaves for healing."*

Ezekiel 47:8-12, NIV

That River is the Holy Spirit or the very presence of God Almighty Himself.

The River of God

In the gospel that bears his name, John tells the story of Jesus meeting a Samaritan woman at the well in her hometown. At that time, the Samaritans were hated by the Jews, who had no dealings with them. Jesus, however, had a very different attitude toward these people.

As Jesus was sitting at the well in Samaria, thirsty from His journey, the Samaritan woman came to the well to draw water. When Jesus asked her to give Him a drink, it took her by surprise. Here was a Jew asking her, a Samaritan, for a drink. Think about that for a moment.

Here was a man who was supposedly her enemy, of those who usually had nothing to do with her ethnic group or race, and yet He was asking her for a drink.

The woman's response was fairly typical and understandable. How was it that a Jewish man was asking for a drink from a Samaritan woman?

But Jesus' response was anything but typical. It was profound, so profound, in fact, that the woman couldn't understand what He was saying. He said:

"If you knew the gift of God, and who it is that asks you for

The River of God

a drink, you would have asked
him and he would have given
you a drink of living water."

John 4:10, NIV

Jesus went on to explain His
words to the woman:

"Every one who drinks this
water [referring to the natural water] *will be thirsty*
again, but whosoever drinks
the water I give him will nev-
er thirst. Indeed, the water I
give him will become in him
a spring of water welling up
to eternal life."

John 4:13-14

That day, before this encounter had ended, the Samaritan woman had tasted of the River of God.

Sometime after this, Jesus was attending a Jewish feast. On the very last day of that feast, when everyone had eaten and drunk to the full, He stood and spoke these amazing words:

If any man thirst, let him come unto me and drink. He that believeth on me as the scripture has said, out of his belly shall flow rivers of living water.   John 7:37-38

The River of God

The scripture Jesus was referring to here was from the book of Deuteronomy. It says:

The LORD your God will raise up for you a prophet like me from among you, from your fellow Israelites.
Deuteronomy 18:15, NIV

The prophet Isaiah had foretold:

Behold God is my salvation, I will trust and not be afraid: for the LORD Jehovah is my strength and my song; he also is become my salvation.

Therefore with joy shall ye draw water out of the wells of salvation.   Isaiah 12:2-3

The beast of the fields shall honour me, the dragons and the owls: because I give waters in the wilderness, and rivers in the desert, to give drink to my people, my chosen.
                    Isaiah 43:20

For I will pour upon him that is thirsty, and floods upon the dry ground: I will pour my spirit upon thy seed, and my blessing upon thine offspring.
                    Isaiah 44:3

The River of God

Come, all you who are thirsty,
come to the waters.

Isaiah 55:1, NIV

King David sang:

There is a river, the streams
whereof shall make glad the city
of God, the holy place of the tab-
ernacles of the most High. God
is in the midst of her, she shall
not be moved.   Psalm 46:4-5

From these passages, we can see and understand how vital the waters of God's River are. They are life to all of us who will willingly drink from them:

For in him we live, and move, and have our being.

Acts 17:28

It is so true, and I am a witness of it. It has worked in my life.

⚄ 2 ⚄

Come to the Water

As the deer panteth for the water brooks, so my soul panteth after thee, O God. My soul thirsteth for God, for the living God. Psalm 42:1-2

To the thirsty, I will give water without cost from the spring of the water of life.
Revelation 21:6, NIV

The Spirit and the bride say, "Come!" And let the one who hears say, "Come!" Let the one who is thirsty come.

Revelation 22:17, NIV

Come unto me all who are weary and heavy laden, and I will give you rest.

Matthew 11:28

As you travel this journey of life, there will come a time when you become weary, tired and thirsty. In the natural, when this happens, you look for something to drink, a place to sit and rest, or a quiet place where you can just relax for a while. So it is with our spirits.

We become tired and thirsty spiritually. Jesus, knowing this, beckons us to come to Him, to come and drink of Him, to come, lay back in Him and find rest.

As a child growing up on the banks of the Bay River, I had the opportunity to enjoy all that the river could offer. I loved the shrimp, crabs and fish but wasn't so crazy about the oysters, clams and scallops (and still am not to this day).

As a child, just playing in the water was a treat. As I noted early on, I enjoyed the fishing and crabbing with Dad. Maybe more than anything else, the river was a place we could go to cool down from the hot, humid summer days. But we couldn't enjoy it if we didn't go there. We didn't live in the river. We had to go there. For me, it was a place I simply "had" to go.

For most of us, childhood is a carefree time. We don't worry about life, but depend on our parents to do all the worrying for us. But then comes adolescence, and we begin to grow up and develop our own agenda and ideas and make our own decisions and choices. Those choices and decisions can (and sometimes do) cloud our spiritual eyes.

Since Dad was a pastor, I grew up in church. It was all I knew from the time I was born. I accepted Christ at the age of eleven and was baptized by my father. It was a good start, for I had come to the River of God. But, after graduating high school and leaving home to attend college, I made a decision that would affect my life for many years to come. I had left the safety and tranquility of the River to pursue my own way.

Over the next fourteen years, I would occasionally go back to church and drink from the River. It wasn't that I didn't know better. As a child, I had learned the ways of God. My parents not only taught me the ways of God, but they also set for me a living example of how to live in His way. Like so many, I had a head knowledge of the River, but my heart was not ready to let go of "my" ways.

Finally, in the latter part of 1978 and early part of 1979, I began to have a hunger and thirst to return to the peace and tranquility of the River. My two older children had been riding a church bus for about a year. The children's church group was having a visitor incentive. If a child brought a visitor, they would receive a little gift. Naturally, in order to satisfy their begging, I said, "Okay, I'll go."

At the time, I was not aware that this was the same church I had attended three years earlier and then sworn to myself that I would never step foot in ever again (I prefer not to say why).

During those three years, there had been a change in leadership at the church, so on Sunday March 4, 1979, I went to church with my children, and my life was turned upside down. I again found that River that my soul and spirit had for so long yearned for. That day Jesus became so real, so personal, and so intimate to me. I had found the true River of Life again. I had returned to that River and decided that was where I wanted to spend the rest of my life.

3

Growing in the River

Until we all reach unity in the faith and in the knowledge of the Son of God and become mature, attaining to the whole measure of the fullness of Christ. Ephesians 4:13, NIV

Even though I had spent years in church and had accepted Christ as my Savior at a young age, I found that I had no idea what a Christian life should be like. I had been a good child and had not gotten into a lot of trouble, but I somehow looked at life with a rather whimsical, care-free attitude.

After graduating from high school and leaving for college, my thought suddenly was, "Now I'm free, and I can do whatever I want." Having grown up in church, I had a certain head knowledge. I had memorized many scripture verses and was excellent of what we called "Sword Drill." It's a group game where a scripture passage is called out and the first one to find it steps forward and reads it. I learned all the Bible stories and could even tell you what they meant. I thought that just being good was all that was needed. I soon began to learn there was a whole lot more to the Christian life than just being good and following the Ten Commandments.

As I began to read and study God's Word, I realized that I had to change, and I was changing. The things I had formerly enjoyed doing no longer seemed so enjoyable. Some of the friends I had been accustomed to hanging out with must have found me dull and boring now, because soon they didn't come around as much or they quit coming altogether. Fortunately, I was beginning to make new friends, a different type of friend.

I have always been an outdoor type person. I loved sports—softball, basketball, football and volleyball. I played them all. I was a member of a women's softball team during the summer of 1979.

During one of the breaks at practice one evening, I was with the team, and most of us were smoking. I had smoked about half of a cigarette when I suddenly decided I didn't want it anymore. I threw it on the ground and stepped on it to put it out. I no longer had a desire for cigarettes.

About three months after that, I decided that I would try another cigarette. That was a BIG mistake, and I have never tried one since. Cigarettes, from that point on, were a thing of the past. It was about a year that I realized God had miraculously delivered me from them.

Thank You, Lord. I had no withdrawals and no temptation

to pick the habit back up, even with a husband who smoked in the house. I was beginning to grow in God's River.

As that first year passed, I found I began to understand more of the Bible. As I would read a certain passage, it seemed as if the passage was talking back to me. God's Word suddenly began to take on a whole new meaning, and I was like a sponge soaking up everything I could get my hands on to read or to listen to that would help me grow in Him.

I was so hungry for more of God. I remember telling my

pastor at the time, "I wish God would take the top of my head off and just pour it all in my brain." He had a good laugh over that and then very gently told me, "It doesn't work that way."

I noticed that my thoughts and desires were changing. I began to see people differently. I was no longer so judgmental. I was learning that you can still love people even if you may not agree with them on some things. You can agree to disagree. I had to tread through murky waters a time or two, but those rough waters made me stronger, and I grew through them.

Now, after nearly thirty years, I can look back and see how, as long as I remained in the River of God, I was changed. There were times when I would just bask on the banks and let my spirit rest and relax. There were other times when I would jump in feet first and just swim and play in the refreshing waters. Then there were the times I would just feast on the manna in the River.

As I stayed in God's River, I grew and became more like Him. To this day, I still depend on the River of God for life, for sustaining health and purpose. Thank God for His River.

4

Life in the River

Consider it pure joy, my brothers and sisters, whenever you face trials of many kinds, because you know that the testing of your faith produces perseverance. Let perseverance finish its work so that you may be mature and complete, not lacking anything. James 1:2-4, NIV

When I first embarked on this new life, I had no clue as to

where I was going or what lay ahead. All I knew was that I was no longer steering the boat. My new Best Friend was on board, and He had the controls.

I read all that I could to learn more about this Best Friend. Like a sponge, I was soaking Him into myself and just couldn't get enough of Him or couldn't learn about Him fast enough. Thankfully, during this time, I had a great pastoral team to help and guide me.

I had grown up in the Original Free Will Baptist Church, and after I got back to God, I called my mother to tell her the good news. I told her not to worry, that I would never leave the Baptist faith and become one of "them," I was referring to the Pentecostals I had heard so much about.

Dad's sister was Pentecostal, and my best friend throughout my schooling was too. I had been to their church on numerous occasions and was vaguely familiar with their beliefs and their very different way of worship. They were not like us Baptists.

I knew a little about the Holy Spirit, but I had been taught that the Baptism in the Holy

Spirit was only for those in the apostolic age, the first-century Church, and not for today. Now, however, as I read and studied the book of Acts, I began to question this teaching.

About two months after I had totally surrendered to Christ, my pastor gave an altar call one Sunday night for anyone who wanted to be baptized in the Holy Spirit to come forward. I made my way to the altar, not really knowing what I was in for, except that I felt eager for everything God had for me.

The pastor's wife and associate pastor's wife both got around me, and we began to praise and thank God and worship Him. It wasn't long before words I didn't know began to flow from my lips, and I began to feel a presence I had never felt before.

I left the service that night a very different person, again embarking on a new journey. When I called my mom, to confess that I was now one of "them" — a Pentecostal, filled with the Spirit and speaking in tongues, she was delighted for me.

This journey was to be, at times, very exciting, but at other times, the waters would seem to be very troubled and rough.

Thank God that He was with me all the way.

For the next two and a half years, I grew and matured in Christ and my new-found faith much more quickly. So far, sailing had been calm and things were going great, but I was about to encounter a tidal wave.

My husband was in the military and decided to put in for a transfer. This was in the summer of 1980. I was still a babe in Christ, and all I knew to do was pray. I must admit that what I prayed was a kind of a selfish prayer, but my heart was sincere. I told God, "I'm not ready to move. I don't know how, but I need You to change these orders." Within two months, my husband, all on his own, decided that was not what he wanted after all and asked to have his orders canceled. Much to our surprise, that request was granted.

Whew! Thank You, Lord.

I was so relieved that God had heard and granted my prayers. Or so I thought. In actuality, our move had only been delayed by a year. One year later, in 1981, my husband received orders to the same duty station as he had the year before. This time he had been asked for by name, which meant there was no was of getting out of it. We were on our way back to North Carolina.

In that year's time, I had grown tremendously in the Lord and although I really didn't want to leave my church and church family, my prayer this time was different: "Father, if this is the plan You have for me, then all I ask is that You give me peace about making the move." I was surprised when that peace came, and I began to actually look forward to moving.

In December of 1981, moving time came. Wonderfully, a family that was going to the church I attended was from the same city we were moving to and had been part of a good Bible-believing church there. The man took me and introduced me to the church and the pastor, and that church made me feel right at home. I was beginning to learn what it was like to live in the River, and it was good.

The waters of life's river were not always smooth, but my Captain and Best Friend was still on board with me, and I knew that no matter what came, I would be okay.

My faith was again put to the test four years later, in 1986.

My husband, who was not a believer, had become an alcoholic and was becoming abusive. I determined that I was not going to live under that type of abuse or have my children grow up in that atmosphere. I made the decision to ask him to leave, and he did—leaving me with the four children to raise on my own.

I lost the home we had just bought the previous year, and I began to question God, my faith and whether or not it was even worth going on in the River. One particular day I had taken the boys to church to go on a Royal Ranger camp-out for the

week-end. Shortly after return-
ing home, I heard a knock on the
door. It was the father of one the
boys who had spent the night
with us the night before. The
boy had left his raincoat, and
the father had come to pick it up
for him. Before he left, he made
a gesture and a remark to me
that was very inappropriate. He
was a married Christian man, a
member of my church, and here
he was making a pass at me. I
was devastated.

When the man left, I sat down
on my couch with my face in
my hands and began sobbing to
God. I told Him that I could not

go on. My world had literally crumbled at my feet.

As I sat there, sobbing to Jesus, I heard a voice singing the words, "With an everlasting love I will love you." I looked up to see Jesus walking through the wall opposite of where I was sitting. He stood there and sang a love song to me, with His arms outstretched.

When the Lord had finished singing that song, He backed out through the same wall He had come in through. He hadn't turned and walked away, but, instead, had backed out, all the while still facing me. That made such an impression on my heart and in my spirit, one I have never forgotten.

This was the Lord's way of reassuring me that He would never turn His back on me. Others might, but not my Lord.

I survived that trauma by holding tight to that visitation and that song and knowing in my knower that Jesus is real and that He would never leave me, no matter what.

In the years that followed, there would come more tests and trials, but I continued in the River. With each test or trial, I would take a plunge in God's

River and there find strength and peace and joy.

My father had passed on to His eternal reward very young in 1969. Then, in 1995, I had a brother who joined Dad in Heaven, and in 2003 my mother joined the two of them. In 2002, I was diagnosed with thyroid cancer and had to have my thyroid removed and to undergo a radioactive iodine treatment.

For the next ten years, the waters were relatively calm. There were some ups and downs and some difficult times, but at least there were no tsunamis. Then came 2013.

That year my only living brother came down with cancer, so my sister went to take care of him. His wife was already in a nursing home with late-stage Alzheimer's. In November of 2013, he joined my parents and brother, and three weeks later to the day, his wife joined them too.

While my sister was down taking care of him, her husband was diagnosed with lung cancer, so she had to go back home to care for him, and in mid December, I went to help her. On Christmas Day, her husband joined the rest of my family, now leaving only two siblings living, me and my sister.

Now my sister sold her house, closing within a month, and on January 31, 2014, we left to drive back to my home in Jacksonville. She had decided to move back to that area too. While we were on our way there, my niece called to tell us that our other brother's wife had joined them in Heaven. In three months, I had lost four family members. You can imagine the deep sadness that gripped me.

Once again, I went to the River of God, and there I found peace and strength. It was my only source, all I had to cling to. I drew from it the same strength and nourishment I had received all these years.

Then, in 2015, my own physical body began to be afflicted. Between 2015 and today, I have had seven major surgeries and a bout with Sepsis, which hospitalized me for eleven days. One thing I am confident of is that I am not alone. As long as I remain in Christ, in His River, I have nothing to fear. Although the waters of life get rough and turbulent, He will keep me safe and will not let me go under.

✍ 5 ✎

Allowing the River to Flow

*Your love, LORD, reaches to the
    heavens,
 your faithfulness to the skies.
    Your righteousness is like
    the highest mountains,
 your justice like the great deep.
    You, LORD, preserve both
    people and animals.
How priceless is your unfailing
    love, O God!*

Allowing the River to Flow

People take refuge in the
shadow of your wings.
They feast on the abundance of
your house;
you give them drink from
your river of delights.
For with you is the fountain
of life;
in your light we see light.
                    Psalm 36:5-9, NIV

A flowing river is a source of
energy which acts on the chan-
nel it flows through to change
its shape and form. A flowing
river is alive. It has a current that
is continually moving. If that
movement stops of gets blocked,

the river will die. It is up to you and me to allow the River of God, His Spirit, to flow in our lives. It is our choice as to how much we allow Him to flow. We can even cause a dam that stops the flow of the waters.

God's River is a never-ending flow of love, a love so deep that our minds cannot comprehend it. It was that love for human kind that caused Jesus to step out of Heaven's glory, to come to this fallen and sin-sick world. It was that love that healed the sick, opened blinded eyes and unstopped deaf ears. It was that love for man that allowed

Jesus to suffer rejection and a brutal beating and death by crucifixion. It was the depth of God's love for you and me that brought Jesus out of the tomb. It is that same River of love that has kept me. This is the love that has given me the ability to keep going when I wanted to give up and quit. That unconditional River of love continues to melt my heart and cause praise and adoration to burst forth from my lips.

This River of God's love has a bountiful supply for whatever is needed in your life. It has healing for the body, mind and soul. It carries provision for life. It brings peace and contentment to a life that is troubled. Everything you need is found in the River of God's love.

God's love for you is so deep that He sent His only Son to earth to die so that you could live. What amazing love!

Looking back over the years, I recall one very special experience that changed my life. It happened in December of 1981. We had just made the move from South to North Carolina and were temporarily spending Christmas with my mother. One day my husband and I were walking through the woods, discussing the move, whether to move on base or off base, where the kids would go to school, etc. We decided to live off base, in town. With me not working, we knew that finances would be tight, but my husband was adamant that he wanted the children to continue in private school.

Without my income now and having to pay for private school for four children, I was not quite sure how we would make it. After all, I had only been living beside the River for two years. I was still a baby Christian. While we were out walking that day, a scripture verse came to mind. It was from Psalm 37:

I have been young and now am old; yet I have never seen the righteous forsaken, nor his seed begging bread. Psalm 37:25

I grabbed hold of that verse, and it became life to me. It was a promise God made that brought encouragement and hope to me at a time when doubt and fear was trying to take over. It was like pulling a great big fish out of the River. That word became sustenance to my spirit and qui-

74

eted my doubts and fears. If God did it for David, He would do it for me too.

We soon found a house and got the children enrolled in private school. Even though our income had been drastically cut and our expenses had almost doubled, we never lacked for a thing. Our bills were always paid on time, even school tuition for four children.

My husband would sometimes look at me and ask how we had done it. All I could say was that it was God and quote that scripture verse back to him. God is faithful to His Word.

Psalm 119:105 tells us:

Thy word is a lamp unto my feet and a light unto my path.

God promises that if we will follow Him, He will light our way and guide our steps. The River of His love is so deep and so rich and is given to each of us freely without measure.

I hope you have found God's River and you will allow this River to flow in your life and let it guide you. I pray that as you do, you will grow and flourish and find peace and content-ment, as I have.

Amen!

www.ingramcontent.com/pod-product-compliance
Lightning Source LLC
Chambersburg PA
CBHW020041040426
42331CB00030B/358